And It Will Be Splendid

And It Will Be Splendid

a guided journal for 2021

CURIOUS CROW BOOKS

First published in 2020 by Curious Crow Books

Victoria Australia

ISBN 978-0-9805249-6-3

Copyright Tor Roxburgh 2020

The moral right of the author has been asserted. All rights reserved. Any person or organisation wanting to copy, store or transmit material contained in this book needs permission in writing from Curious Crow Books.

Design, illustration and typesetting: Holly Dunn

www.torroxburgh.com

Welcome to this journal

Dear Fellow Traveller,

Welcome to 'And It Will Be Splendid'!

I hope this year really is splendid for you. I hope it brings you joy and harmony, good health, great friends, and lots of creative energy and fun.

I prepared this guided journal during the pandemic of 2020. I haven't mentioned COVID19 in the writing prompts because… Because I couldn't predict the future and I didn't want to fill your journal with the virus. I love to think the pandemic will have disappeared by the time you read this, but I suspect 2021 will be another year to take care of your health and the health of those in your community.

I used to think that journaling was all about choosing someone to write for. Now I think the important thing is recording your life: your small and intimate life and your bigger life – as it entangles and disentangles with the world around you.

You will find two types of prompt for each week of the year:

The creative prompt invites you to explore life beyond your daily routine.

The second prompt is relatively simple and invites you to write about what happened, where, and with whom.

Feel free to respond to either or both and to alter the prompts to suit your mood. If you're enjoying writing and need more room, grab a notebook and keep going.

I hope this journal brings you pleasure. If you have suggestions for next year's journal please include them in your review on Amazon, Goodreads or your preferred online review platform or social media app.

Your sister in journaling,

Tor Roxburgh

PS – I hope the Australian/UK spelling conventions don't drive you crazy if you're living in the United States. Hopefully, you come to love 'neighbourhood' and 'labour' and all the other 'u' inclusions.

January

A month for creative prompts about reflecting and resolving

28 Dec 2020 - 3 Jan 2021

You are probably itching to get into your journaling process. The prompts for this week and the next two weeks can be switched about depending on your inclination. This week's is about looking back to 2020. The next focuses on grand plans for 2021. The third invites you to consider making exquisite small plans for the year.

Creative Prompt: There are lots of aspects of 2020 that you may be happy to farewell and never see again. This week's prompt invites you to write about the clever things you did that you want to bring forward as well as the things you are never going to do again. Describe what made the year hard and what helped make things easier.

_____
_____
_____
_____
_____
_____
_____
_____
_____
_____
_____
_____
_____
_____
_____
_____
_____

The Week: What happened this week? Did you celebrate or snuggle down at home? Describe what you have been doing.

4 Jan - 10 Jan 2021

Creative Prompt: This week's prompt invites you to make some grand plans. Making grand plans is fun. It's also an opportunity to play with tenses. Last week you probably wrote "I was" and "I am". This week your inclination might be to write "I will" but consider this: acting as though your grand plans have already been realised can make them easier to achieve. It's like trying on clothes, buying them, and wearing them when you leave the shop.

Make a list of your grand plans and put yourself into them in the present or the past tense. You might write: "I have moved house" or "I am in love" or "My saxophone brought me plenty of gigs in 2021" or "I have written my memoir".

The Week: What has been happening with your finances this week? Think back on what you have bought and the bills you have paid. Do any changes need to be made?

11 Jan - 17 Jan 2021

Creative Prompt: Grand plans are lots of fun and their stories keep us motivated and focused on the future. Trouble is, we live our lives in the present and most of our pleasure comes from attending to modest goals like going out to dinner, listening to music, and playing with pets or children. When you list some of your modest goals for the new year try using the same trick that you used last week: write in the past tense or the present tense. You might write: "I love walking the dog after lunch each day" or "I am listening to music in the evenings" or "I rang a friend for a chat each week in 2021".

The Week: Who have you spent most of your time with this week? Describe the relationship.

18 Jan - 24 Jan 2021

Creative Prompt: This week's prompt invites you to reflect on your values and the influence they have on your life. Which values do you hold sacred? Which values are important to you? Which values do you admire or reject? Drawing on your actions in 2020 and the first month of 2021, make some connections between your values and your behaviour. Are you happy with what you have discovered? Do you want to add to your New Year's resolutions?

The Week: What small things did you attend to this week? List some of the modest tasks you undertook and the shortest conversations you had.

25 Jan - 31 Jan 2021

Creative Prompt: Imagine yourself in a parallel word where almost everything matches this world. There is one key difference between the two and you get to choose what that difference is. Choose something that would make your life more interesting in the parallel world. There is only one catch: the difference isn't allowed to be about wealth or money.

The Month: The past five weeks included the end of the old year and the first weeks of the new. What was the month's emotional tone? Were you happy with the conversations you had and the actions you took?

February

A month for creative prompts about people and personalities

1 Feb - 7 Feb 2021

Creative Prompt: It's always lovely looking back and reading descriptions of the people in your life. This week's prompt invites you to start with someone in your outer circle. Pick an acquaintance who interests you and describe them as though they were a character in a book or movie.

The Week: Where have you been this week? Have you walked anywhere? Have you been out of the house? What places have you visited?

8 Feb - 14 Feb 2021

Creative Prompt: Go wide this week and describe the stranger who had the greatest impact on your life in during 2020 and this year. You might choose a national or global leader. You might write about someone more local such as a city official or local journalist. What are they like and why did you choose to write about them?

The Week: What happened in the big wide world this week? Pick some of the events that you believe are significant.

15 Feb - 21 Feb 2021

Creative Prompt: This week's prompt invites you to describe the most important person in your life other than yourself (That's for next week!). Paint a picture of that person and recall an instance: choose a time when they did or said something memorable or important. Journaling about someone's words and actions creates a cinematic feel and brings personalities to life on the page.

The Week: What have you been doing in your domestic life this week? Describe a typical moment in your homelife.

22 Feb - 28 Feb 2021

Creative Prompt: This week's prompt focuses on the main character in your story: YOU!

Take a mental step back and look at yourself from the outside. Use some kindness and love when you introduce yourself. What do you look like? What sort of things could we expect to see you doing and saying? Use the technique you used last week and create that cinematic feel.

_____
_____
_____
_____
_____
_____
_____
_____
_____
_____
_____
_____
_____
_____
_____
_____
_____
_____
_____
_____
_____
_____
_____
_____

The Month: The end of February can feel as though it arrived too soon. We only just started the year and yet we're two months in. What happened in your life this month? Don't forget to include the good things, even if they are small.

March

A month for creative prompts about things and stuff

1 Mar - 7 Mar 2021

Creative Prompt: Our objects and the meanings they carry can make fascinating reading. This week's prompt invites you to journal about the things in your wallet. Open it up and spread out any cash, any cards, any coins, and any mementos and documents. Describe what is there and what it all means.

The Week: What happened in your family this week? Don't forget that 'family' can mean whatever you want it to mean.

8 Mar – 14 Mar 2021

Creative Prompt: Look down and notice what you are wearing. Why are you wearing what you are wearing? Take a quick trip to your closet and look at what's inside. Are you happy with what you see? Are your clothes comfortable and aligned with your vision for yourself and your resolutions for the year?

The Week: What have you been doing this week? If you divided up your week, what has taken most of your attention?

15 Mar - 21 Mar 2021

Creative Prompt: Take a little walk inside your home and look at all the objects around you. Which items have snuck into your life uninvited? Which things have you chosen? Which objects do you dislike? What have you had to compromise about? Pick a couple of objects and write their story.

The Week: What have you been talking about this week? Describe the conversations that have excited, saddened or angered you.

22 Mar - 28 Mar 2021

Creative Prompt: This week's prompt invites you to write about an object in your neighbourhood. Step outside and take a little walk or drive around. Notice the things you like and dislike. Choose something to journal about. Write about it as though you are seeing it on a movie screen and then explain its meaning.

The Month: If you would like a second chance to create New Year's Resolutions, this is the moment. The Roman year originally began in March with January and February added some time later. In any event, it's a good moment to review the start of the year and refine your resolutions.

April

A month for creative prompts about friendships and relationships

29 Mar - 4 Apr 2021

Creative Prompt: Do you have a best friend right now? If not, why not? Is it a choice or have you been finding it hard to connect? Describe your current favourite friend (and that may not be your best friend). Explain why you are enjoying that person now.

The Week: What have you been thinking about this week? Write down some of your internal dialogues.

5 Apr – 11 Apr 2021

Creative Prompt: What do you have in common with your friends? What are the differences between you and the people you socialise with? Do the differences make the relationships interesting – or hard to manage? Are there any patterns in the friends you choose?

The Week: What have you been feeling this week? Describe what has been going on in your heart.

12 Apr - 18 Apr 2021

Creative Prompt: This week's prompt invites you to reflect on the friendships in your childhood. Describe one of your childhood playmates and explain the joys and disappointments that relationship brought you. Describe how that friendship ended or lasted as you grew.

The Week: What have you been up to this week? Focus on actions rather than feelings. Describe what you have been doing.

19 Apr - 25 Apr 2021

Creative Prompt: It's hard to imagine living a life without having experienced a friendship breakup. Look back and reflect on the end of a friendship. Use kindness and distance when describing that person and everything that happened. What did you learn?

The Month: For many people this month will have featured faith-related events. April includes the end of Pesach (the Jewish Passover festival), the Christian festival of Easter, Ram Navami (the Hindu celebration of Lord Rama's birthday), the Chinese Qingming Festival (Tomb-Sweeping Day), Baisakhi (the Sikh New Year), and the start of Ramadan (the Islamic month of fasting and prayer) among other events. What were your events this month? Were they secular or religious?

May

*A month for creative prompts about playing
and wondering*

26 Apr - 2 May 2021

Creative Prompt: Write your life as a poem or a string of poetic sentences. Let yourself loose and be as arty and florid and sentimental as you like. If you like rhyme, try rhyme. If not, you might like to head in the opposite direction and keep things tight and arrhythmic.

The Week: Who have you been talking to this week? What have you been saying and how have others been responding?

3 May - 9 May 2021

Creative Prompt: This week's prompt invites you to think about portraits and paintings of historic events. If you had to paint your portrait what would it look like? Where would you be sitting or standing? What colours would feature? If you had to paint an historic scene from your life, what would we see?

The Week: What have you done in the evenings this week? What have you been reading or watching or thinking about?

10 May - 16 May 2021

Creative Prompt: Turn your thoughts to music. Go to your playlists, CDs or records. Play some of the songs or pieces you feel like listening to right now. Why do you like them? What do they evoke? What memories do they hold? If May were a song, which would it be?

The Week: What have you been eating and cooking? List some of the meals you've enjoyed and the people you've shared them with.

17 May - 23 May 2021

Creative Prompt: Describe your life as a metaphor. Your life could be an oak tree. It could be a game of football. It could be a tapestry. It could be a house. It could be anything. Try using "I am" or if it's easier "he/she is…". Explain your chosen metaphor.

The Week: Have you been looking after someone or has someone been looking after you? Has everything involved self-care? Describe the caring in your life that has been going on this week.

24 May - 30 May 2021

Creative Prompt: Write a fairy tale about your life or a life you've watched. Start with "Once upon a time" and borrow some of the elements from the stories of childhood. The elements could include journeys, transformations, magical objects, meeting mentors, crossing thresholds and more.

The Month: The season is almost over: spring is about to become summer in the Northern Hemisphere and autumn will turn to winter in the Southern Hemisphere. What has the month been like where you live and what have you been doing?

June

A month for creative prompts about truth and power

31 May - 6 Jun 2021

Creative Prompt: This week's prompt invites you to journal about what you like to do. The truth about your preferences may have been papered over in the years between childhood and today. What activities brought you simple pleasures as a child? Do today's activities bring you the same sort of joy? Describe any changes you want to make.

The Week: How was your working week? Were you working in the home or outside the home? How did you feel about your achievements and tasks?

7 Jun - 13 Jun 2021

Creative Prompt: This week's prompt invites you to reflect on your power.

You might have some control over other people: children, workers, customers, or clients. You might have control over an environment. Power can also be internal. Are you acting powerfully in your life? Are you using your full creative and organisational capacity or are you holding back and feeling hesitant? Use some examples from your life to journal about your relationship to power.

The Week: How are the younger members of your family and friendship circle? Did you speak with any of them this week? Have you journaled about them this year?

14 Jun - 20 Jun 2021

Creative Prompt: This week's prompt invites you to write about being influential this year.

Last week you were invited to consider power, which is about control. Influence is more subtle. You have probably influenced lots of people this year. You may have influenced them directly or indirectly. Your influence could have been intentional or unintentional. Did you enjoy the feeling of influence and was it based on something positive or negative in your life?

The Week: What have you been thinking about this week? Describe your thoughts as a chain of ideas and explain the way this influenced your actions.

21 Jun - 27 Jun 2021

Creative Prompt: The world outside your life is full of different ideas about what is true and false. Pick two of the most contentious ideas from 2021 and journal about them. Describe your position on the issues and work out whether you have based your beliefs on solid prejudice or solid ground.

The Month: You are halfway through the year. Take a moment to review the past six months and weigh them against your expectations for 2021. Do you need to adjust your resolutions and ambitions, or do you need to change the world around you?

July

A month for creative prompts about nature and nurture

28 Jun - 4 Jul 2021

Creative Prompt: Take yourself outside this week. Leave your home. Your journey might take you from your sitting room to your balcony. It might take you out into the wilderness. Write about your senses: what do you see, hear, smell, touch? Is there a taste in the air?

The Week: How are you feeling this week? Are you happy with your emotional journey throughout the week? Describe what's happened.

5 Jul - 11 Jul 2021

Creative Prompt: This week's prompt invites you to engage in a writing exercise. Choose a landscape that is dear to you and describe it without using any punctuation. Let one thing run into another. Try using words like 'and', and 'but' and 'then' to join your thoughts. It may feel odd at first, but you'll end up with something that is strangely poetic.

The Week: What have you been wondering this week? Are there things that you wish you knew? Did you go hunting for information? Did you find it?

12 Jul - 18 Jul 2021

Creative Prompt: This week's prompt invites you to journal about nurturing. Are you nurturing something or someone? You might be cultivating a garden, bringing up a child or educating a pet. Describe the way you are approaching the task. What are you focusing on? What's your philosophy?

The Week: Where have you spent most of your time this week? Set the scene and describe why you were in that place.

19 Jul - 25 Jul 2021

Creative Prompt: Last week's prompt invited you to journal about nurturing others. This week's prompt asks you to write about looking after yourself. Describe your approach to caring for your wellbeing. What have you learnt about the things you need? Has this year been different from last year? Do you need to avoid some experiences, and do you need to incorporate others?

The Month: It is mid-season: summer in the Northern Hemisphere and winter in the Southern Hemisphere. Journal about some of your classic July activities.

August

*A month for creative prompts about
imagining and speculating*

26 Jul - 1 Aug 2021

Creative Prompt: If you could have a day in someone else's life, whose life would you choose? Describe that person and explain why you would like to experience their life. Is there anything you share with that person? Is there a habit you could cultivate or an attitude you could adopt that would bring that person's essence into your life?

The Week: How are the older members of your family and friendship circle? Has the year been hard on them? Did you speak with any of them this week? Have you journaled about them this year?

2 Aug - 8 Aug 2021

Creative Prompt: If you suddenly found out there were only two months left in the world, what would you do? Describe your thought process and explain your decisions. Journal about the values that drove those decisions.

What did you learn? Is there anything useful or joyful that you could bring into your real life?

_____
_____
_____
_____
_____
_____
_____
_____
_____
_____
_____
_____
_____
_____
_____
_____
_____
_____
_____
_____
_____
_____

The Week: How is your community doing this week? Describe the group of people around you that make up your community and write about some of their challenges, advantages, disadvantages, and strengths.

9 Aug - 15 Aug 2021

Creative Prompt: This week's prompt invites you to imagine packing just one suitcase and departing your home forever. You might be heading for Argentina, Mars, or a lifetime at sea – but you're not coming home again. Think through your possessions and decide what to pack. Will you take objects, clothes, food, books, plants, or something different? Explain your choices.

The Week: What brought a smile to your face this week? It may have been a fleeting thought or an image online. You might have heard something happy or remembered something nice.

16 Aug – 22 Aug 2021

Creative Prompt: Imagine that you have a second chance at life. You don't get an exact re-run but you will meet similar challenges, opportunities, and difficulties – and there will be some familiar characters. If you had to place a bet, what are the key decisions and situations for which you should prepare? Write about them and take note of any lessons for your life right now.

The Week: Where have you been this week? Has life kept you indoors, at your desk, on your tools or out and about? Write about your environment and how you feel about it.

23 Aug - 29 Aug 2021

Creative Prompt: In the second week of August the creative prompt invited you to think about the world ending. This week's prompt asks you to consider an excessively long life. Imagine that you will live to be 140. Imagine you will remain in good health. Imagine this longevity is an absolute certainty. Describe what you would do in the next five years to prepare for the long road ahead.

The Month: What have you been wondering this month? Describe some of the events, opportunities and ideas that have caught your attention.

September

A month for creative prompts about listening and learning

30 Aug - 5 Sep 2021

Creative Prompt: This week's prompt invites you to listen to some of your own stories. What are the best and worst tales you've told yourself? Describe how the stories arose and look at how truthful they actually are. Were they helpful to you? Did you enjoy them? Are you still listening to them? Are they wearing you out?

The Week: How are your finances doing this week? Is this time of year easy or difficult financially and what are your thoughts about budgeting for the end of year holiday season?

6 Sep - 12 Sep 2021

Creative Prompt: Consider your relationship with learning. Think back and recall the feeling of excitement when you picked up something new. In childhood you may have felt that spark when learning to read or write or play a sport. Later in life you may have felt it when learning to drive or to speak another language. That experience of excitement can sometimes disappear over time. What are you doing this year to keep that spark alive?

The Week: How are your relationships this week? Describe who you are living with or keeping in close contact with. Are you enjoying any intimacy? Do you wish they would come a little closer or move further away?

13 Sep - 19 Sep 2021

Creative Prompt: This week's prompt invites you to explore a calling. If there is a "calling" then there must be someone who hears – and is ready to listen. Have you felt yourself called to do something this year? It doesn't have to have a religious connotation, but it might. Describe the closest you have come to that sensation in 2021 and how you have responded.

The Week: What has come into your life from the outside world this week? Has a new task emerged? Have you heard from someone, unexpectedly? Have family members or friends been in touch?

20 Sep - 26 Sep 2021

Creative Prompt: Our minds have a store of other people's stories that we have listened to over the years. Often with older family members those stories are on repeat. Choose one of the oft-heard stories, take a step back, and listen to it afresh. Is there another way of hearing that story? If you can, and if you want to, ring the person and ask some different questions.

The Month: Where have you been walking this month? Perhaps you've been walking into the past. Maybe you have been exploring the physical world or the spaces in your home or workplace. What have you seen and what sense did you make of it?

October

A month for creative prompts about rituals and routines

27 Sep - 3 Oct 2021

Creative Prompt: This week's prompt invites you to journal about rituals. On a superficial level a ritual is a customary way to celebrate. On a deeper level it can help us achieve transcendent states. What are the rituals that were practised in your family when you were growing up? Which rituals have you kept alive and carried into your current life? Describe the times when rituals lifted you beyond your daily experience. And if there are none, what could you try this year?

The Week: What have you done to relax this week? Describe some of your moments of rest. Journal about unwinding and loosening yourself from the daily grind.

4 Oct - 10 Oct 2021

Creative Prompt: Think about the secular rituals of your adolescence. Did you spend hours grooming and dressing? Did you put on music before going out? Did you ring or text a friend before going to sleep at night? Do some of those habits linger? Do some of them need to be revived?

The Week: What have you touched this week? Your hands might have been busy in a kitchen or on a computer keyboard or in a garden. You may have touched others: in a loving or caring relationship.

11 Oct - 17 Oct 2021

Creative Prompt: Some of the rituals of childhood relate to ideas about cause and effect and the possibility of magic. Dig deep into the past and recall some of your personal rituals: some may have been family rituals; others may have been secret.

Did you prepare food for Santa? Did you leave teeth for the tooth fairy? Did you jump over cracks? Are you still jumping over cracks?

The Week: How have you spent your time this week? Work out how much time you have given to all your different tasks and make a rough pie chart. Do you like what you see?

18 Oct - 24 Oct 2021

Creative Prompt: The routines of your daily life are probably quite practical and sensible. You will have a way of doing things, a process you enjoy, a method that saves you time and energy. Routines can be beautiful things. This week's prompt invites you to consider your bodily routines. Think about getting up, bathing, getting dressed, eating, exercising, and sleeping. Describe one or two of your happiest routines. If you're not happy with your habits, pick a small one to spark a change.

The Week: What about your grand plans for 2021? Have you brought them to mind this week? Are you still invested in your ideas from January? If they need a tweak, do it now.

25 Oct - 31 Oct 2021

Creative Prompt: Routines are part of your working life too. If you are working in the home your routines may have a long lineage shared with a parent or a grandparent – or you may have created them afresh. If you work outside the home your routines might be part of a corporate lineage. Describe some of your most and least favourite routines. If you don't like them, are you able to change them?

The Month: What has happened in your life this month? Has it been more of the same or has your life been interrupted by events? Describe everything that has been going on in your world and include the people in your family or your friendship circle. Don't forget to describe people's actions and words and appearance as though you are seeing them on a movie screen. It will bring them to life on the page.

November

A month for creative prompts about emotions and expressions

1 Nov - 7 Nov 2021

Creative Prompt: This week's prompt invites you to consider the people you love.

When you think of family or your circle of friends is there anyone who brings extra warmth to your soul? Think about that person for a moment and try and recall a particular incident or action that shows something about what you value in them.

The Week: What have you been looking at online this week? Have you enjoyed or learnt from what you've seen? Has it added a layer of meaning in your life or is it a way to escape the world?

8 Nov - 14 Nov 2021

Creative Prompt: This time of year can sometimes provoke feelings of jealousy as you speculate about the lives, habits and cultures in other homes, families and workplaces. Have you felt envy this year? Describe how you have managed to unwind those feelings.

The Week: What have your conversations been about this week? Have you been speaking to anyone about anything that matters? Is the talk about feelings or about pragmatic issues and transactional arrangements?

15 Nov - 21 Nov 2021

Creative Prompt: This week's prompt invites you to journal about feeling inspired. It's a much-loved emotion that is motivational, optimistic, and future orientated. Look back over your week and find a couple of little sparks of inspiration. What were they? What did you do when you felt them? Are you a "tell everyone about your ideas" communicator or a silent "nurture it first" type? Are you happy with the way you work with inspiration?

The Week: What were your daily routines this week? Is life continuing as normal or has the lead up to the holiday season interfered with your regular habits?

22 Nov - 28 Nov 2021

Creative Prompt: In a season when emotions can run high it is interesting to focus on how you express your feelings. Last week's prompt invited you to journal about how you express your moments of inspiration. This week's asks you to consider the way you express some of the other emotions. What are you like when you love someone? Write about how fear emerges. How do you behave when you're feeling sad, lonely, joyful, or grateful?

The Month: Where are you this month? Take a moment to draw a picture of your physical world. You might take an overview and write about your neighbourhood or you might focus on a room where you've spent much of your time.

December

A month for creative prompts about preparing and pausing

29 Nov - 5 Dec 2021

Creative Prompt: Your thoughts might well be tuning in to 2022.

It's often hard to focus on anything much in the rush towards the end of the year, but this week might offer a little oasis for projecting into the New Year. Another year brings excitement, but it can be tinged with regret if too many of your ambitions for 2021 remain unrealised. Be a kind to yourself as you consider using this week to take stock of now and imagine the future.

The Week: Who have you had contact with this week? Have you been with friends or family or colleagues or children? Have you connected with others in person or have you been in touch remotely?

6 Dec - 12 Dec 2021

Creative Prompt: Describe the arrangements you have made for the holiday season. Who will you see? Will you be avoiding anyone? Will you be avoiding everyone? What will your family or circle of friends be doing? Are you happy with what you have organised? Describe the approach you have taken and reflect on any tweaks you might like to make.

The Week: What have you been listening to this week? You might have listened to music or audio books. You may have been listening when others talk or listening to yourself. What have you heard that has touched your heart?

13 Dec - 19 Dec 2021

Creative Prompt: This week's prompt invites you to consider preparing yourself for the relationship avalanche that the holiday season often involves. Sometimes the challenge is all about not having enough people in your life or not having the type of people you want to have in your life. If this describes your experience, try journaling about your plans to look after yourself. Even when relationships are good and you have plenty of people to celebrate with, the volume of interactions can be exhausting. If this describes your situation try journaling about your plans to build some protective strategies into the week ahead.

The Week: What have you felt this week? Describe this week's emotional journey using examples.

20 Dec - 26 Dec 2021

Creative Prompt: This week's prompt invites you to journal about the small moments – those minutes and seconds when you took a deep breath and remembered to relax your body and mind. When did that happen? What prompted any moments of solace? If you haven't been having any quiet moments, you might want to write about looking for some quiet time next week.

The Week: What have you been eating and cooking? Describe some of your kitchen and dining room moments. Has this been a good week for food? Did you enjoy what you ate?

27 Dec 2021 - 2 Jan 2022

Creative Prompt: Take a little lie down on the couch before you start writing. Rest your body and let you mind float across the months of 2021. What bubbles up? Describe any surprisingly wonderful moments. Write about the sad things too. You might need to venture into a second notebook if there is a lot that you want to journal through. Consider making a list of thoughts you want to carry into 2022.

The Month: You are on the threshold again. Think about this past month. Describe two interesting ideas, two conversations (including with yourself), two transcendent moments where you experienced a self-realisation, and two belly laughs. Focus on the good and happy moments that you would like to carry forward into 2022.

About the author

Tor Roxburgh is the author of more than 16 books and has taught non-fiction writing at the University of Melbourne. She trained in philosophy and has a background in the creative arts and publishing, as well as professional writing and editing. Tor has worked extensively in the community, supporting and inspiring teenagers and adults to fulfil their writing dreams.

Find out more by subscribing to Tor's newsletter at www.torroxburgh.com or follow Tor on social media.

If you have suggestions for next year's journal please include them in your review on Amazon, Goodreads or your preferred online review platform or social media app.